AMAZING ANIMALS OF THE WORLD ②

Volume 3

Cricket, European Mole — Frog, Agile

GROLIER

First published 2005 by Grolier, an imprint of Scholastic Library Publishing

For information address the publisher: Grolier, Scholastic Library Publishing
90 Old Sherman Turnpike
Danbury, CT 06816

Set ISBN: 0-7172-6112-3; Volume ISBN: 0-7172-6115-8

Printed and bound in the U.S.A.

Library of Congress Cataloging-in-Publications Data:
Amazing animals of the world 2.
p.cm.
Includes indexes.
Contents: v. 1. Adder—Buffalo, Water -- v. 2. Bunting, Corn—Cricket, Bush -- v. 3. Cricket, European Mole—Frog, Agile -- v. 4. Frog, Burrowing Tree—Guenon, Moustached -- v. 5. Gull, Great Black-backed—Loach, Stone -- v. 6. Locust, Migratory—Newt, Crested -- v. 7. Nuthatch, Eurasian—Razor, Pod -- v. 8. Reedbuck, Mountain—Snake, Tentacled -- v. 9. Snakefly—Toad, Surinam -- v. 10. Tortoise, Gopher—Zebu.
ISBN 0-7172-6112-3 (set : alk. paper) -- ISBN 0-7172-6113-1 (v. 1 : alk. paper) -- ISBN 0-7172-6114-X (v. 2 : alk. paper) -- ISBN 0-7172-6115-8 (v. 3 : alk. paper) -- ISBN 0-7172-6116-6 (v. 4 : alk. paper) -- ISBN 0-7172-6117-4 (v. 5 : alk. paper) -- ISBN 0-7172-6118-2 (v. 6 : alk. paper) -- ISBN 0-7172-6119-0 (v. 7 : alk. paper) -- ISBN 0-7172-6120-4 (v. 8 : alk. paper) -- ISBN 0-7172-6121-2 (v. 9 : alk. paper) -- ISBN 0-7172-6122-0 (v. 10 : alk.paper)
1. Animals--Juvenile literature. I. Title: Amazing animals of the world two. II. Grolier (Firm)
QL49.A455 2005
590--dc22

2005040351

About This Set

Amazing Animals of the World 2 brings you pictures of 400 fascinating creatures and important information about how and where they live.

Each page shows just one species—individual type—of animal. They all fall into seven main categories or groups of animals (classes and phylums scientifically) that appear on each page as an icon or picture—amphibians, arthropods, birds, fish, mammals, other invertebrates, and reptiles. Short explanations of what these group names mean, and other terms used commonly in the set, appear on page 4 in the Glossary.

Scientists use all kinds of groupings to help them sort out the thousands of types of animals that exist today and once wandered here (extinct species). Kingdoms, classes, phylums, genus, and species are among the key words here that are also explained in the Glossary (page 4).

Where animals live is important to know as well. Each of the species in this set lives in a particular place in the world, which you can see outlined on the map on each page. And in those locales the animals tend to favor a particular habitat—an environment the animal finds suitable for life, with food, shelter, and safety from predators that might eat it. There they also find ways to coexist with other animals in the area that might eat somewhat different food, use different homes, and so on. Each of the main habitats is named on the page and given an icon/picture to help you envision it. The habitat names are further

defined in the Glossary on page 4.

As well as being part of groups like species, animals fall into other categories that help us understand their lives or behavior. You will find these categories in the Glossary on page 4, where you will learn about carnivores, herbivores, and other types of animals.

And there is more information you might want about an animal—its size, diet, where it lives, and how it carries on its species—the way it creates its young. All these facts and more appear in the data boxes at the top of each page.

Finally, you should know that the set is arranged alphabetically by the most common name of the species. That puts most beetles, say, together in a group so you can compare them easily.

But some animals' names are not so common, and they don't appear near others like them. For instance, the chamois is a kind of goat or antelope. To find animals that are similar—or to locate any species—look in the index at the end of each book in the set (pages 45-48). It lists all animals by their various names (you will find the giant South American river turtle under turtle, giant South American river, and also under its other name—arrau). And you will find all birds, fish, and so on gathered under their broader groupings.

Similarly, smaller like groups appear in the set index as well—butterflies include swallowtails and blues, for example.

Table of Contents
Volume 3

Glossary

Amphibians—species usually born from eggs in water or wet places, which change (metamorphose) into a land animal. Frogs and salamanders are typical. They breathe through their skin mainly and have no scales.

Arctic and Antarctic—icy, cold, dry areas at the ends of the globe that lack trees but see small plants grown in thawed areas (tundra). Penguins and seals are common inhabitants.

Arthropods—animals with segmented bodies, hard outer skin, and jointed legs, such as spiders and crabs.

Birds—born from eggs, these creatures have wings and often can fly. Eagles, pigeons, and penguins are all birds, though penguins can't fly through the air.

Carnivores—they are animals that eat other animals. Many species do eat each other sometimes, and a few eat dead animals. Lions kill their prey and eat it, while vultures clean up dead bodies of animals.

Cities, Towns, and Farms—places where people live and have built or used the land and share it with many species. Sometimes these animals live in human homes or just nearby.

Class—part or division of a phylum.

Deserts—dry, often warm areas where animals often are more active on cooler nights or near water sources. Owls, scorpions, and jack rabbits are common in American deserts.

Endangered—some animals in this set are marked as endangered because it is possible they will become extinct soon.

Extinct—these species have died out altogether for whatever reason.

Family—part of an order.

Fish—water animals (aquatic) that typically are born from eggs and breathe through gills. Trout and eels are fish, though whales and dolphins are not (they are mammals).

Forests and Mountains—places where evergreen (coniferous) and leaf-shedding (deciduous) trees are common, or that rise in elevation to make cool, separate habitats. **Rainforests are different (see below).**

Fresh Water—lakes, rivers, and the like carry fresh water (unlike Oceans and Shores, where the water is salty). Fish and birds abound, as do insects, frogs, and mammals.

Genus—part of a family.

Grasslands—habitats with few trees and light rainfall. Grasslands often lie between forests and deserts, and they are home to birds, coyotes, antelope, and snakes, as well as many other kinds of animals.

Herbivores—these animals eat mainly plants. Typical are hoofed animals (ungulates) that are common on grasslands, such as antelope or deer. Domestic (nonwild) ones are cows and horses.

Hibernators—species that live in harsh areas with very cold winters slow down their functions then and sort of sleep through the hard times.

Kingdom—the largest division of species. Commonly there are understood to be five kingdoms: animals, plants, fungi, protists, and monerans.

Mammals—these creatures usually bear live young and feed them on milk from the mother. A few lay eggs (monotremes like the platypus) or nurse young in a pouch (marsupials like opossums and kangaroos).

Migrators—some species spend different seasons in different places, moving to where more food, warmth, or safety can be found. Birds often do this, sometimes over long distances, but others types of animals also move seasonally, including fish and mammals.

Oceans and Shores—seawater is salty, often deep, and huge. In it live many fish, invertebrates, and even some mammals, such as whales. On the shore birds and other creatures often gather.

Order—part of a class.

Other Invertebrates—animals that lack backbones or internal skeletons. Many, such as insects and shrimp, have hard outer coverings. Clams and worms are also invertebrates.

Phylum—part of a kingdom.

Rainforests—here huge trees grow among many other plants helped by the warm, wet environment. Thousands of species of animals also live in these rich habitats.

Reptiles—these species have scales, lungs to breathe, and lay eggs or give birth to live young. Dinosaurs are thought to have been reptiles, while today the class includes turtles, snakes, lizards, and crocodiles.

Scientific name—the genus and species name of a creature in Latin. For instance, Canis lupus is the wolf. Scientific names avoid the confusion possible with common names in any one language or across languages.

Species—a group of the same type of living thing. Part of an order.

Subspecies—a variant but quite similar part of a species.

Territorial—many animals mark out and defend a patch of ground as their home area. Birds and mammals may call quite small or quite large spots their territories.

Vertebrates—animals with backbones and skeletons under their skins

European Mole Cricket
Gryllotalpa gryllotalpa

Length: 2 inches
Number of Eggs: 100 to 300
Home: native to Eurasia and North Africa; introduced elsewhere

Diet: mainly insects and insect larvae; also earthworms
Order: Grasshoppers and their relatives
Family: True crickets

  Cities, Towns, and Farms

 Arthropods

© BRUNO ROTH / OKAPIA / PHOTO RESEARCHERS

The European mole cricket is a master tunneler. This creature is well designed for this line of work. Its front legs are shaped like shovels, helping it to dig through the soil. The cricket's heavy shield protects the top and sides of the animal's thorax. The upper parts of its abdomen are also sturdy. At the end of the abdomen are two long appendages called cerci, which pick up vibrations in the soil and help the cricket locate insects and other prey.

Mole crickets live almost exclusively in the burrows they build. As they build their tunnels, they bite through roots and other underground, or subterranean, plant parts. In doing so, they can cause much damage to gardens. Young mole crickets even eat tiny roots until the crickets are big enough to prey on small invertebrates.

The male European mole cricket "sings" with his wings in order to attract a mate. The edges of his wings are rough where they overlap. When the cricket rubs the edge of one wing against the edge of another, a low, whirring sound is produced. After mating, the female lays her eggs in a special underground nursery chamber. Her tasks consist of guarding the eggs against enemies and licking the eggs often to keep them clean. The eggs hatch in two to four weeks. The babies stay in the nursery for several weeks until they begin to explore the rest of their underground world.

Mormon Cricket
Anabrus simplex

Length: 1 to 2¾ inches
Diet: plants
Number of Eggs: 60 to 150
Home: North America

Order: Grasshoppers and their relatives
Family: Katydids

 Cities, Towns, and Farms

 Arthropods

© ALLAN MORGAN / PETER ARNOLD, INC.

Although it looks like a cricket, the stout Mormon cricket is actually a katydid, a type of grasshopper with very long antennae. The Mormon cricket got its name in 1848. During that year, thousands of these katydids attacked the first crops planted in Utah by the Mormon pioneers. Fortunately, a huge flock of California gulls arrived in time to eat most of the insects before they could destroy all the pioneers' crops. The Mormon cricket continues to be a pest today. However, since Mormon crickets can't fly, farmers can protect their crops with walls and pit traps dug in the ground.

Normally, Mormon crickets feed in high, rugged hills on wild herbs. But when food is scarce, young Mormon crickets begin to gather in large bands to migrate. These swarming katydids start traveling on warm, sunny, and windless days. Moving in a straight line, they can cover a distance of up to a mile a day. They crawl and tumble over all kinds of objects and are often described as quite clumsy. On cool days and at night, the migrating katydids seek shelter and wait. When temperatures rise above 65 degrees Fahrenheit, the Mormon crickets resume their march. Swarming Mormon crickets can be very destructive. They may consume entire fields of grain and have a special liking for wheat and alfalfa. Mormon crickets can also ravage a vegetable garden in a single day.

6

Red Crossbill
Loxia curvirostra

Length: 5½ to 6½ inches
Wingspan: 10 to 11 inches
Weight: about ¾ ounce
Diet: seeds of pine, spruce, and other conifers

Number of Eggs: 3 to 5
Home: North America, Central America, Europe, and Asia
Order: Perching birds
Family: Finches

Forests and Mountains

Birds

© TIM ZUROWSKI / CORBIS

The red crossbill is a very aptly named bird. The upper and lower halves of the bird's red bill cross, a unique arrangement that makes the bill the perfect utensil for opening up the cones of pines and other evergreen trees. When the red crossbill locates a pinecone, it hops on top of the cone, rips off the scales with its bill, and removes the seeds with its tongue. When pinecone seeds are in short supply, the red crossbill dines on the insects that are so abundant in its home forests of North America, Central America, Europe, and Asia.

Red crossbills breed early in the year, when snow still blankets the ground. The female builds a cup-shaped nest in a tree near the edge of a forest. She uses twigs, bark, and small roots, and lines the nest with soft grass, moss, and feathers. Meanwhile, the male keeps her company as she flies back and forth with the nesting materials. The male red crossbill's real work starts when his mate incubates the eggs—he must feed not only himself but also bring food back to the female.

Within two weeks the eggs hatch. Crossbill chicks are born with their eyes closed tight and their bill straight. Both parents feed the crossbill chicks until the young leave the nest, about three weeks after hatching. In a short while, the bill grows crooked and crosses—just in time for the arrival of pinecone season!

American Crow
Corvus brachyrhynchos

Length: 17 to 21 inches
Wingspan: 33 to 40 inches
Weight: about 1 pound
Diet: insects and other small invertebrates; garbage; corn and other seeds

Number of Eggs: 3 to 7
Home: North America
Order: Perching birds
Family: Crows, jays, and magpies

 Cities, Towns, and Farms

 Birds

© TIM ZUROWSKI / CORBIS

The jet-black American crow is a common sight throughout most of the United States and Canada. Its "caw-caw" call is also very well known, as is its talent for mimicking chicken squawks, dog whines, and even human words and laughter. The crow is a very adaptable bird, living in woodlands, grasslands, farmlands, suburban gardens, and many other habitats.

The American crow eats just about anything: insects, spiders, snails, frogs, small snakes, baby birds, and earthworms. Crows that live near water grab clams and sea urchins, carry them high into the sky, then drop them on rocks to crack open the shells. Crows are also scavengers, feeding on garbage and dead animals, especially creatures killed by cars. Crows eat seeds, too. They often visit cornfields, especially in fall, to feed on corn left behind after harvesting. The harm to crops caused by crows is far surpassed by the benefits gained from the crows' enormous consumption of cutworms, grasshoppers, and other insect pests.

American crows usually build their nests in trees and bushes. The nest is made of twigs and branches, and is lined with soft plant fibers, moss, and other materials. The eggs are incubated for 18 days. Baby crows begin to fly when they are about a month old. Crows that live in Canada and the northern United States migrate southward in fall.

Carrion Crow
Corvus corone corone

Length: about 20 inches
Weight: about 1¼ pounds
Diet: dead animals, small mammals and birds, eggs, frogs, mollusks, insects, worms, and vegetable matter

Number of Eggs: 4 to 6
Home: Europe
Order: Perching birds
Family: Crows, jays, and magpies

 Cities, Towns, and Farms

 Birds

© MANFRED DANEGGER / NHPA

Carrion crows eat just about anything they can find, although they prefer a diet of flesh. They are quick to attack wounded birds and other small animals, which they stab with their heavy black beak. They also feed on dead animals, or carrion. To open mollusks, walnuts, or other hard-shelled foods, this intelligent bird drops them from the air so that the impact of hitting the ground cracks open the shell.

The all-black carrion crow, *Corvus corone corone*, lives in Central Europe and Great Britain. It is often seen along the edges of forests and in farm fields and meadows, but it will even venture into city parks if left undisturbed. Generally the carrion crow feeds while hopping over open ground, either singly or in pairs. Its close relative, the hooded crow (*C. c. cornix*), is gray and lives in Ireland, Italy, Asia, and the Middle East. The two species interbreed wherever their populations meet.

Carrion crows mate for life. The pair nests in the fork of a tree or on the ledge of a cliff. They build a sturdy nest of dry, broken twigs that they patch together with mud and moss. The nest is lined with grass, fur, and other soft materials. The female warms the eggs until they hatch. Both parents bring food to the chicks until the youngsters are old enough to fly. The family usually stays together until winter. Most carrion crows remain in the same place year-round rather than migrate to warmer climates.

Fish Crow
Corvus ossifragus

Length: 16 to 20 inches
Wingspan: 30 to 43 inches
Weight: 14 to 15 ounces
Diet: shellfish, bird and turtle eggs, insects, and berries
Number of Eggs: 4 or 5

Home: Atlantic and Gulf coasts of North America
Order: Perching birds
Family: Crows, jays, and magpies

 Oceans and Shores

  Birds

© TIM ZUROWSKI / CORBIS

The fish crow looks much like its bigger cousin, the common crow. But, unlike the common crow, the fish crow prefers seafood and life near the water. Fish crows always live either in coastal areas such as beaches and saltwater marshes or inland near swamps and large rivers. They enjoy company and live in groups that may have thousands of members.

Fish crows eat many different foods, but they prefer seafood. They hunt for their favorite delicacies along the shore or in shallow water, searching for crabs, shrimp, crayfish, and small fish. The fish crow gets many of its best meals by robbing other birds! It often dives toward more timid gulls and terns, scaring them into dropping whatever food they have caught. Fish crows will also steal eggs from the nests of other birds. For variety, they sometimes dine on berries, ants, and grasshoppers. Fish crows also provide a service to cattle by eating ticks that land on their back.

When nesting time arrives, the fish crow finds a tall tree, preferably with a waterside location. There the bird constructs its nest with sticks and twigs, and lines it with pine needles, animal hairs, and other soft materials. While the female is incubating the eggs, the male hunts and brings food back to feed his mate. The eggs are incubated for about 16 days. The male and female fish crow share the work of feeding and raising their fast-growing young.

Dace
Leuciscus leuciscus

Length: up to 1 foot
Diet: insects, worms, freshwater crustaceans, and larval fish
Home: Eurasia

Method of Reproduction: egg layer
Order: Carps and their relatives
Family: Minnows

 Fresh Water

 Fish

© HANS REINHARD / BRUCE COLEMAN INC.

Dace are found in streams and rivers throughout Europe and Asia, and gather in small schools near the water's surface. When they meet danger, an entire school can change course as if it were a single fish. There is no one leader directing the school's movement. Each dace coordinates its movements with its neighbors using a special sense organ called a Weberian apparatus. With this organ, dace can literally hear each other move in the water and can instantly react to changes in course.

Dace breed from March through May. During this time the females get round and fat. The males grow large white warts on their body. These changes help the dace recognize members of the opposite sex.

After breeding, the female deposits her eggs on underwater plants.

The dace's many predators include large fish such as perch and trout. Many predatory birds such as kingfishers and herons depend on the dace for food. The fish is quite common throughout much of Europe. It has several closely related cousins that are abundant in Russia and parts of Asia. But in the United States, many dace species are in danger of extinction. These endangered species all live in small freshwater habitats that are easily damaged by pollution and human development. The endangered fish include the desert dace and the Clover Valley specked dace, both of Nevada, and the Kendall Warm Springs dace in Wyoming.

Blue-green Darner
Aeschna sp.

Length: 2¼ to 3¼ inches
Diet: butterflies and other insects
Method of Reproduction: egg layer
Wingspan: 3 to 4 inches

Home: Europe, Africa, Asia, and the Americas
Order: Dragonflies and damselflies
Family: Darners

 Fresh Water

 Arthropods

© STEPHEN DALTON / PHOTO RESEARCHERS

The blue-green darner is a large dragonfly that has a dark-colored body with blue markings. When the creature flies into the sunlight, its body often looks green. Typically the male has a green-and-yellow head and blue-green eyes. The female's head is yellow, and she has blue eyes.

The darner is named after the darning-needle shape of its long, slender body. This insect usually lives near ponds and swamps. It is most abundant in Europe, but several species can be found near North American ponds.

Adult blue-green darners tend to be active from midsummer until the end of September. In some years, they may appear as early as June and live until the end of October. Like other dragonflies, the darner hunts like a hawk, soaring over lakes, ponds, and canals in search of prey. Sometimes it makes a quick dash over dry land, searching for insects on open paths and lanes. It often stops to sun itself on shrubs and bushes.

To mate, the male darner grabs the female behind her head, using the claspers on his belly. The two often mate piggyback in midflight. What looks like a stinger on the female's tail is really an "ovipositor." She uses it to cut slits in water plants or to make holes in mud. She then deposits one egg in each slit or hole.

Green Darner
Anax junius

Length: 2⁷⁄₁₀ to 3⅕ inches
Diet: mosquitoes, flying insects, and small fish
Method of Reproduction: egg layer
Wingspan: 4⅕ inches

Home: North America, Hawaii, and the east coast of Asia
Order: Damselflies and dragonflies
Family: Dragonflies

 Fresh Water

 Arthropods

The big green darners once carried the nickname "devil's darning needles" because it was popularly believed that they sewed shut the ears of naughty schoolchildren. The story wasn't true, of course. In fact, darners, a type of dragonfly, do not even sting.

The green darner has a green thorax, two pairs of transparent wings, and a bluish abdomen. The largest and fastest of the dragonflies, it often ventures far from water, flying at between 35 and 65 miles per hour. They can detect movement from 40 feet away.

Early in the year, the darners fly about in search of prey. Their favorite food is honeybees, which they capture in flight. As the mating season approaches, the males establish territories. Darners often fly in tandem for long periods when mating. In the quiet waters where they breed, females insert their eggs into the stems of aquatic plants. The newly hatched young, called naiads, have long, smooth bodies and long legs to help them climb though submerged plants and debris. Their large lower lip is equipped with a pair of hooks that can be shot out in front of the head. Once these hooks have seized prey, they retract into the mouth. This adaptation enables the naiads to catch tadpoles and small fish. Darners are eaten by fish and birds.

Axis Deer (Chital)
Axis axis

Length: 3½ to 4½ feet
Height at the Shoulder: 2½ to 3 feet
Weight: 165 to 220 pounds
Diet: grass, leaves, and fruit

Number of Young: 1
Home: India and Sri Lanka
Order: Even-toed ungulates
Family: Deer

  Forests and Mountains

Mammals

© RODER TIDMAN / CORBIS

The chital, or axis deer, is the largest species of wild deer in India. Its stocky body is covered with brown spotted fur—spots that give the creature still another name, the Indian spotted deer. Chitals are native to India and the island of Sri Lanka, and they have been introduced to other lands as well.

The head of the chital is short, its eyes large, and its tail medium to long (8 to 12 inches). The chital's antlers are unique, with each having three graceful branches. Unlike most deer that have a seasonal antler cycle, the chital grows and sheds antlers throughout the year. The chital remains close to rivers, where it flees to escape its enemies. Chitals travel in large herds noted for the hierarchy that develops among the males. The strongest males stay at the center. Around them are the females and the fawns, while at the edge stand the weaker males and those males that have just shed their antlers.

The chital has been observed spending a good portion of the day under trees where langur monkeys feed, eating items that the monkeys have rejected. Together the two animals protect one another from such enemies as the tiger and the leopard. The monkey uses it keen eyesight to see the enemy from its treetop home, while the deer can detect predators through its strong sense of smell.

Chinese Water Deer
Hydropotes inermis

Length of the Body: about 3 feet
Length of the Tail: about 3 inches
Weight: about 30 pounds
Diet: grasses, beets, and other vegetables

Number of Young: 1 or 2
Home: China and Korea; introduced to Europe
Order: Even-toed hoofed mammals
Family: Deer

 Forests and Mountains

 Mammals

© ROLAND SEITRE / PETER ARNOLD, INC.

The male Chinese water deer is quite unique. Instead of antlers the stag has 3-inch-long fangs. During breeding season, full-grown stags engage in bloody duels. The battling males swing their heads at one another's neck and shoulders, allowing their sharp fangs to gouge out chunks of hair and skin. They continue fighting until one flees or lies flat on the ground in defeat. Even outside of breeding season, a large stag will not tolerate other males within his territory.

As its name suggests, the Chinese water deer lives in a very wet habitat. Many live along the banks of China's Chang Jiang River. Other populations are found in swampy lowlands in China and Korea. These deer often hide in tall marsh grasses and reeds. To avoid discovery, they stand very still for long periods of time if necessary.

This sandy-colored deer is a solitary creature. However, a stag will allow one or more does to share his territory. He marks the borders of his "property" by rubbing his forehead against tree trunks and other objects, leaving behind his scent. Although these deer are not social, they do vocally warn each other of danger.

Most of what we know about the Chinese water deer is from observing individuals kept in zoos. In Europe the captive deer mate in spring. Six months later the females give birth. Although a litter of one or two fawns is typical, there may be as many as six.

Fallow Deer
Dama dama

Length: 4½ to 5¼ feet
Height at the Shoulder: 3 feet
Weight: 70 to 185 pounds
Diet: grasses, leaves, and other plant matter
Number of Young: 1 or 2

Home: Europe and Iran; introduced elsewhere
Order: Even-toed hoofed mammals
Family: Deer

Forests and Mountains

Mammals

© KEVIN SCHAEFER / CORBIS

Many European parks and forests are graced by groups of fallow deer. And groups you usually see—these gregarious animals spend most of their time together. During much of the year, groups consist of females and their young. Adult males live by themselves in smaller groups, and old males, called stags, often live alone. Despite their apparent friendliness to each other, the fallow deer is a shy animal. Although it has excellent vision and very good senses of smell and hearing, it flees at the slightest sign of danger. As it runs, it holds its black-edged tail upright.

Like most deer, only the male sports antlers. He sheds the antlers each year, after the mating season, and then grows a new set. Antlers make very handy weapons, especially during the fall mating season, when males fight among themselves. The male also uses his antlers to protect himself against wolves and other predators.

The fallow deer sheds its coat twice a year. The summer coat is a light reddish brown with white spots. The winter coat is dark brown and very thick. Some fallow deer have coats of different colors.

The female fallow deer, or doe, gives birth to one or two young in spring. The baby, called a fawn, usually weights between 4½ and 9 pounds at birth. Fallow deer have a life span of 20 to 25 years.

Pampas Deer
Ozotoceros bezoarticus

Length: 4 to 5 feet
Height at the Shoulder: 2 to 2½ feet
Weight: about 80 pounds
Diet: grasses, herbs, and leaves

Number of Young: 1
Home: South America
Order: Even-toed hoofed mammals
Family: Deer

 Grasslands

Mammals

© THEO ALLOFS / VISUALS UNLIMITED

? Endangered Animals

The pampas deer is a small, playful species that once roamed widely across the South American pampas, or grassland. Today only small, scattered herds survive. Unfortunately, evolution did not design this beautiful deer for the onslaught of civilization. Hunters found the deer easy to kill by taking advantage of its curious nature. Pampas deer investigate anything unusual in their habitat. Hunters quickly learned they could lure the deer by simply waving a bright handkerchief. Domestic dogs have also killed countless pampas deer. In addition, entire herds have died from diseases spread by domestic sheep and cows.

Among themselves, pampas deer are quite gentle and peaceful. Bucks often engage in play fights, but real battles are rare. All bucks—young or old, weak or strong—are free to wander from one small herd to another. The herds are not territorial. Generally these creatures live in small groups. Larger herds gather over newly burned areas of the pampas in order to feed on the tender sprouts of new grass.

Mating occurs from December to April. The mated female gives birth about six months later to a small spotted fawn. The mother keeps her baby hidden in tall grass until it is strong enough to run with the herd. When a pampas deer is frightened, it warns its neighbors by stamping, whistling, and releasing a foul-smelling odor from its feet.

17

Red Deer
Cervus elaphus

Length of the Body: 5½ to 8 feet
Length of the Tail: 5 inches
Height at the Shoulder: 4 to 5 feet
Weight: 155 to 480 pounds
Diet: plant matter

Number of Young: 1
Home: Europe and Asia; introduced elsewhere
Order: Even-toed hoofed mammals
Family: Deer

 Forests and Mountains

Mammals

© ROBERT PICKETT / CORBIS

The male red deer well deserves its nickname "king of the forest." This dignified creature even has a crown of sorts—a regal set of bony antlers that look like the intricate branches of a tree. The antlers may be more than 4 feet long, with as many as 60 points. While growing, the antlers are covered with a hairy skin called velvet. After about 100 days, when the antlers have fully grown in, the velvet dries. The deer rubs his antlers on trees or rocks to remove the velvet—a process called polishing.

During the mating season, each male establishes a territory and tries to attract as many females as possible. This premating ritual often leads to conflicts between males over female red deer. The fighting can be bloody, with these usually gentle animals ramming each other headfirst, often inflicting skin wounds and damaging their antlers. After mating season ends, the males shed their antlers, only to regrow them the following fall. Without antlers the deer must rely on their strong hooves for defense against predators.

Red deer have excellent senses of sight, sound, and smell. When they sense danger, they quickly run away. For safety's sake, these creatures usually live in small groups. After all, five pairs of watchful eyes, sharp ears, and sensitive noses are better than one!

Dhaman
Ptyas mucosus

Length: about 8 feet
Diet: rats, birds, and other small animals
Method of Reproduction: egg layer

Home: India, Ceylon, Afghanistan, China, and Java
Order: Lizards and snakes
Family: Colubrid snakes

 Rainforests

 Reptiles

© ASHOK JAIN / NATURE PICTURE LIBRARY

The bold dhaman, also called the Indian rat snake, is a familiar visitor to the villages and farms of Southeast Asia. As it races after its prey, this aggressive snake does not hesitate to rush into an inhabited hut or stable. It hisses and barks with a rough, coughlike sound as it attacks. Although a speeding, barking snake can be quite frightening, people welcome the dhaman because it is an efficient pest killer with a taste for rodents.

Amazingly fast and agile, the slender dhaman races up tall trees in pursuit of its prey. This powerful climber glides skillfully from one branch to the next. It often attacks birds at the very top of the rainforest canopy.

The dhaman's speed also makes it difficult to catch. But skillful snake handlers trap dhamans and use them in performances. In India, snake charmers occasionally display the dhaman as a substitute "cobra." Dhamans do resemble cobras superficially. Both snakes can coil their neck into an "S" shape and flatten and inflate their neck into a broad fan. In some parts of India, native people believe that dhamans are male cobras. Actually the two snakes are not closely related. An important difference: the dhaman is not venomous. Although it bites its prey to capture it, the dhaman kills by squeezing and suffocating the victim. The snake then swallows its prey whole.

African Wild Dog
Lycaon pictus

Length: 2½ to 3⅓ feet
Height: 2 to 2½ feet
Weight: up to 65 pounds
Diet: carnivorous
Number of Young: 2 to 10

Home: savannas of Africa south of the Sahara
Order: Carnivores
Family: Dogs

 Grasslands

 Mammals

© DAVE HAMMAN / GALLO IMAGES / CORBIS

? Endangered Animals

The African wild dog lives on the grassy plains of Africa. With its large, erect ears and blotched coat of black, yellow, and white fur, it looks somewhat like the hyena. Some people even call it the "hyena dog." Its bushy tail, though, is more like the tail of a fox.

The African wild dog is a fierce hunter. These dogs hunt in packs of from 6 to 20 animals, although some packs have been seen with as many as 90 dogs. Racing at speeds of about 30 miles per hour, they catch and kill gazelles, antelopes, and even zebras. They usually hunt during the morning, late afternoon, or early evening, avoiding the heat of the midday sun. While hunting, they keep in touch with each other through sounds much like birdcalls. At other times, however, they may bark, growl, or even whimper, just like household pets. Packs of African wild dogs are well-organized. While some of the dogs hunt, others watch over the young, especially those that are too small to leave their dens. The dogs make their dens in the underground nests abandoned by other animals. African wild dogs can give birth to 10 or more pups.

The greatest enemies of the African wild dogs are lions and people. But while the animals usually flee from lions, they are not afraid of humans and do not attack them. Countless African wild dogs have been shot to death, and they have disappeared from many populated areas.

20

Spiny Dogfish
Squalus acanthias

Length: 28 to 40 inches
Diet: small fish, squid, shrimp, sea anemones, jellyfish, and algae

Number of Young: 6
Home: oceans worldwide
Order: Dogfish sharks
Family: Dogfish sharks

Oceans and Shores

Fish

© JOYCE PHOTOGRAPHICS / PHOTO RESEARCHERS

Like wild dogs on land, spiny dogfish hunt in packs in the sea. These small sharks devour large numbers of herring, salmon, and other valuable commercial fish. They also tear at fishing nets and bite off bait and hooks from fishing lines.

The spiny dogfish serves many useful purposes, however. Many Europeans consider the dogfish good eating. There it is made into fish-and-chip dinners. The spiny dogfish's skin is covered with tiny bumps, called "denticles," which gives it the feel of fine sandpaper. When dried, the skin can be used to polish wood or as a rough kind of leather. In North America, many high school students know the spiny dogfish from

biology class. The shark's body is often dissected during anatomy lessons.

The spiny dogfish has two long spines on its dorsal fins. These spines probably discourage larger fish from biting. The spiny dogfish's enemies include humans, swordfish, and larger species of shark.

Although not endangered, the spiny dogfish is becoming rare. The species may not be able to recover well from overfishing, because it reproduces slowly. Adult females give birth only once every two years. The newborn are often eaten by larger fish. Young dogfish also mature very slowly and do not have babies of their own until they are six to 20 years old.

Eccentric Sand Dollar
Dendraster excentricus

Height: ¼ inch
Width: 3 inches
Method of Reproduction: egg layer
Home: West Coast of North America

Diet: tiny food particles removed from sand and mud on the ocean floor
Order: Sand dollars
Family: Dendrasterids

  Oceans and Shores

Other Invertebrates

© NORBERT WU / PETER ARNOLD, INC.

People are probably more familiar with the eccentric sand dollar when it is dead than when it is alive. The attractive lime shells of these creatures are often washed ashore on the West Coast of North America after the animal has died. The shells are circular, very flat, and look like large white coins. Some people call them "sea cookies."

When the eccentric sand dollar is alive, its flattened body is covered with many short spines. If any of the spines break off, the animal grows, or regenerates, new ones. The spines are movable. The sand dollar uses them to move along the sea bottom. The spines also help push sand containing food toward the mouth, which is located in the center of the animal's lower surface.

Eccentric sand dollars live on the sandy seafloor in bays and in the open ocean, from the low-tide line to a depth of about 130 feet. Adult eccentric sand dollars do not swim, but rather, live mostly buried in the sand. During the reproductive season, females release eggs into the water. Then males release sperm. The eggs and sperm mingle in the water, and fertilization takes place. A fertilized egg develops into a larva that swims about for several weeks. Then it sinks to the seafloor and changes its shape. It develops a shell and looks like a tiny sand dollar.

Pacific White-sided Dolphin
Lagenorhynchus obliquidens

Length: up to 6½ feet
Weight: 220 to 330 pounds
Diet: mainly squid and fish such as anchovies and hake
Number of Young: 1

Home: temperate waters of the North Pacific Ocean
Order: Whales, dolphins, and porpoises
Family: True dolphins

  Oceans and Shores

Mammals

© BRANDON COLE / VISUALS UNLIMITED

Pacific white-sided dolphins live in huge groups that may contain 1,000 or more individuals. They often swim together with other species of dolphins and even with gray whales and humpback whales. Pacific white-sided dolphins are excellent swimmers and move swiftly and gracefully through the waters of the North Pacific Ocean.

The most distinctive feature of a Pacific white-sided dolphin is the hooked fin on its back. The upper parts of the dolphin are black and gray; the underside is white. The animal's genus name, *Lagenorhynchus*, comes from two Greek words meaning "bottle" and "beak." The name refers to the shape of the dolphin's forehead and snout.

Under the skin of a white-sided dolphin is a layer of oily fat called blubber. This fat insulates the body and helps the dolphin float. Its nostrils are on the top of its head and open through a blowhole. This makes it easier for the dolphin to breathe without coming too far out of the water.

Pacific white-sided dolphins feed at night. They migrate with the seasons—or, more correctly, with the anchovies that are an important part of their diet. In summer and fall, the dolphins follow anchovies into coastal waters. In fall and winter, they chase the anchovies into deeper waters. The main enemies of these dolphins are killer whales, sharks, and people.

Laughing Dove
Streptopelia senegalensis

Length: 10¼ to 11 inches
Number of Eggs: 2
Home: Africa, the Middle East, and Southwest Asia

Diet: mainly seeds
Order: Pigeons, doves, and their relatives
Family: Pigeons and doves

 Grasslands

 Birds

© PETER JOHNSON / CORBIS

Near the villages and farms of Africa and the Middle East, flocks of laughing doves gather to eat fallen seeds. This small dove's soft coo is a hurried five-note song: "doo-doo doooh-doooh doo." The third and fourth notes are slightly longer and higher in tone. The whole giggling phrase sounds somewhat like the laugh of a shy, young child.

In addition to having a cheery song, the reddish-brown laughing dove is quite handsome. It looks similar to the turtledove, but can be distinguished by its darker feathers and a pretty blue badge across the center of each wing. The laughing dove also flies slower and with more effort than does the graceful turtledove.

Like the pigeons of American and European cities, the laughing dove can become very tame. It is most common in the populated parts of its range, from small desert oases to large city parks. In the Middle East, the bird is also known as the palm dove, because of its habit of gathering in palm groves. Laughing doves do especially well in areas such as Saudi Arabia, where people bring water and crops into the desert. The laughing dove's natural habitats, however, are thorny forests and savannas with scattered trees.

In the wild, laughing doves nest in bushes and trees from 4 to 18 feet off the ground. In populated areas, they often nest on houses and the ledges of buildings.

Oriental Water Dragon
Physignathus cocincinus

Length: about 31 inches
Diet: insects, small animals, and fruits
Method of Reproduction: egg layer

Home: Southeast Asia
Order: Agamids and chameleons
Family: Agamids

 Rainforests

 Reptiles

© DOMINIQUE DELFINO / PETER ARNOLD, INC.

At first glance the oriental water dragon looks like a slightly smaller version of the familiar green iguana of South and Central America. Like the iguana the water dragon is bright green with shades of blue around its throat. It also has a frill of comblike spines that runs down the center of its back. But these two species, living half a world away from each other, are not closely related. They have evolved similar bodies and play similar roles in their separate rainforest homes. An oriental water dragon can be distinguished from the iguana by the large crest on its head. It also has an especially long brown-striped tail.

The oriental water dragon lives near water, in the thick woods and jungles of Southeast Asia. When danger approaches, the creature quickly dives beneath the water surface for refuge. It is a strong swimmer, even in rapidly flowing rivers. In the morning the water dragon sunbathes on large branches that overhang the water. Generally this lizard lives alone or with a mate. The males are territorial and fight with other males that trespass within their home ranges.

Water dragons can be kept as pets in large aquaterrariums. They require dry sand, water, and plenty of sturdy things to climb on. For food, they will accept cat food and lean meat, but prefer a diet of live mice and worms.

Torrent Duck
Merganetta armata

Length: 15 inches
Diet: insects and their larvae
Number of Eggs: 2 to 5
Home: South America

Order: Ducks and screamers
Family: Swans, geese, and ducks

 Fresh Water

 Birds

© ERIC AND DAVID HOSKING / CORBIS

The torrent duck swims like a fearless and expert canoeist. At home in the rushing streams of the Andes Mountains, this duck climbs waterfalls and crashing rapids, and shoots downstream again. As it rides the rushing current, the torrent duck bobs wildly, rolls over, and almost disappears in the foam and spray of the river.

To help keep a grip on slippery rocks and steep ledges, the torrent duck has sharp claws. It also uses its long, stiff tail much like a third leg. On the front shoulder of each wing, the torrent duck has a bony spur, which may help it scramble upstream.

Torrent ducks have not been well studied in the wild, because they live in such remote mountainous areas. From what little

we know, these ducks stop to mate in the calm eddies of a river or stream. The courting pair circle each other, snapping their bills. After breeding, the male and female make a nest in a hole along the riverbank. They stay together and share in the care of both eggs and young. This shared child rearing is unusual among dabbling ducks, the group to which this species belongs.

Not long after they are born, the tiny torrent ducklings jump into the wild water behind their parents and zoom downstream. Like their parents, the ducklings have a narrow, soft bill that they use to probe for fly larvae under and between the river rocks.

Dunlin
Calidris alpina

Length: 7 to 9 inches
Diet: insects, spiders, worms, mollusks, and small crabs
Number of Eggs: 2 to 4
Egg Length: 1 to 1½ inches

Home: coastlines of the Northern Hemisphere, including the Arctic
Order: Waders, gulls, and auks
Family: Sandpipers

 Oceans and Shores

 Birds

© NIALL BENVIE / CORBIS

This common sandpiper is sure to catch your attention if you walk too close to its nest. Dunlin parents will swoop and flutter over the head of a beachcomber, trilling their rhythmic song. For, as long as you're peering up at their acrobatics, these protective parents can be sure you won't spot their eggs. The nest is probably hidden in the grass just beyond the sandy shore. If you were to carefully sneak a peek, you might see several blue-green eggs speckled with red and brown, lying on a small bed of dried leaves and lichen.

Female dunlins often migrate much farther south in winter than do their mates. To get a head start on this journey, the females often leave their half-grown chicks alone or in the care of the fathers. The chicks often join a later flock at the end of the summer.

After a winter holiday in Mexico and Central America—or in North Africa, if these were European dunlins—the birds return north in spring. Some fly all the way past the Arctic Circle to nest along the north shore of Alaska, the Yukon, and the Northwest Territories. Chances are that you will see the same dunlins at the same spot along the same beach each year. These shorebirds form a lifelong attachment to the first nest site they choose as adults. This strong fondness for the "old neighborhood" is usually enough to reunite a dunlin couple year after year.

27

Magnificent Feather Duster
Sabellastarte magnifica

Length: about 5 inches
Diet: plankton and dissolved plant and animal matter
Method of Reproduction: egg layer

Home: Gulf of Mexico, Caribbean Sea, and Bahamas
Order: Sedentary polychaetes
Family: Fan worms

 Oceans and Shores

 Other Invertebrates

ROYALTY-FREE / CORBIS

Feather-duster worms are named for their plume of featherlike gills and tentacles. The largest species in American Atlantic waters is the magnificent feather duster. It wears a crown of 48 frilly tentacles that can extend four inches or more from the worm's central mouth. This plume of "feathers" is exceptionally colorful, with many bands of purple, red, and brown.

The body of the feather duster worm is encased in a strong, leathery tube. Like the stem of a plant, this tube is "planted" in sand or gravel, or wedged into a tiny crevice. Magnificent feather dusters remain in shallow water. There they catch tiny bits of dissolved food with their slightly sticky tentacles. The food rolls down the tentacles and into the worm's mouth. Like other feather dusters, this species quickly withdraws its feathery crown when disturbed. However, it can regrow some or all of its tentacles if they are torn away.

Feather dusters breed by spewing out clouds of eggs and sperm. They spawn in this way in the morning, when the first rays of sunlight glimmer through the water. Shortly after spawning, many adults shed their tentacles. In this way, they avoid eating their own newly hatched larvae. Despite their exotic beauty, magnificent feather dusters are hardy creatures. For this reason, they are popular additions to marine aquariums.

Slime Feather Duster
Myxicola infundibulum

Length: up to 8 inches
Weight: 1 ounce
Diet: phytoplankton and
zooplankton
Number of Eggs: 300 to 700

Home: Mediterranean Sea,
Atlantic Ocean, and the
English Channel
Order: Tube worms
Family: Fan worms

 Oceans and Shores

 Other Invertebrates

© ANDREW J. MARTINEZ / PHOTO RESEARCHERS

With its violet fan spread like a peacock strutting its plumage, it's no wonder that the slime feather duster is considered one of the most elegant of all marine worms. Its flowerlike fan is equipped with light sensors. Wave your hand over a slime feather duster, and the shadow will cause it to snap closed in a flash. The worm withdraws its fan with a powerful set of retractor muscles. In this way, it avoids being eaten by passing fish.

The adult feather duster's fan is the only part of its body that moves quickly—or at all. When just a young polyp, the slime feather duster encases itself in a thick tube. This body armor may extend as far as 8 inches beneath the sand. Thus anchored in place, the creature will remain in one spot for the rest of its life. Only the top of its tube and the colorful fan remain on display.

This creature's slimy appearance comes from a sticky liquid that it squirts onto its fan to help snag food particles floating in the water. It earns the name "feather duster" from the tiny, featherlike hairs that gently brush these bits of food down grooves in the fan toward the feather duster's mouth.

Like other fan worms, the slime feather duster uses its fan not only to eat but also to breathe. The fan contains gills, similar to a fish's, which draw water into special cells that extract oxygen from the water.

29

Tawny Eagle
Aquila rapax

Length: 26 to 31 inches
Weight: 4½ to 8½ pounds
Diet: carcasses and small animals
Number of Eggs: 1 to 3

Home: Eastern Europe, Asia, and Africa
Order: Birds of prey
Family: Hawks and their relatives

 Grasslands

 Birds

© JOE MCDONALD / BRUCE COLEMAN INC.

The tawny eagle is a predator, a scavenger, and a pirate. Flying over grasslands and high steppes, it literally drops onto squirrels, hares, and other prey. It also ambushes small animals by waiting outside their burrows. Tawny eagles are often the first birds at a carcass. As for piracy, tawny eagles often steal food from other birds of prey—snatching it right from their claws or beak.

In Asia the tawny eagle is known as the steppe eagle. Steppe eagles are somewhat larger than the tawny eagles of Europe and northern Africa. Both species have ragged dark brown plumage. Tawny eagles are often confused with similar species such as golden, imperial, and spotted eagles.

However, tawnies lack the majestic, soaring movements of their cousins.

Tawny eagles first mate when they are four to seven years old. Typically the pair builds a mound of straw on the ground, a low bush, or a pile of stones. The female warms the eggs while her mate brings food. Although three eggs may be laid, only the oldest or strongest chick survives, usually because it kills its weaker brothers or sisters.

Over the past 100 years, tawny eagles have greatly decreased in number, largely because farmers have plowed under their grassland habitats. The good news is that these eagles remain abundant in areas between the Volga and Ural rivers in Russia.

Long-nosed Echidna
Zaglossus bruijni

Length: 18 to 35 inches
Height at the Shoulder: 16 inches
Weight: 11 to 22 pounds

Diet: earthworms
Home: New Guinea
Order: Monotremes
Family: Echidnas

 Forests and Mountains

 Mammals

© DANIEL HEUCLIN / NHPA

Not surprisingly, the long-nosed echidna is named for its long, downward-curving snout. Although peculiar-looking, this snout, with a small circular mouth at the end, helps the echidna feed most efficiently.

At night the animal comes out of its underground burrow and hunts for earthworms on the floor of the New Guinea forest where it lives. The echidna's long tongue, which itself looks like a worm, is kept sticky by saliva and acts like flypaper. When the echidna spots a worm, it shoots out its tongue and—zap—pulls its dinner into its mouth!

Although the long-nosed echidna's thick body is covered with soft brown or black fur, don't let this cuddly appearance fool you! Hidden in the fur are dangerously sharp spines. These short spines are used to defend the echidna against predators—principally people, who hunt it for food. Another way people harm the long-nosed echidna, a way against which it cannot defend, is to cut down the forests where the animal lives. No one knows how many long-nosed echidnas remain on the island of New Guinea, or if the species is in danger of extinction.

The long-nosed echidna is related to the Australian echidna, but, as its name indicates, its snout is longer than that of its cousin. It also has shorter front claws than its Australian relative.

Conger Eel
Conger conger

Diet: other fish, crustaceans, and the carcasses of dead animals
Method of Reproduction: egg layer

Length: up to 8 feet
Home: all oceans except the eastern Pacific
Order: Eels
Family: Conger eels

 Oceans and Shores

 Fish

© SOPHIE DE WILDE / JACANA / PHOTO RESEARCHERS

The flesh of the conger eel is delicious to eat. But fishermen catch this eel only accidentally—and usually regret it! The vicious conger eel is as hard to kill as it is dangerous. After sinking its teeth into its enemy, the eel twists and thrashes violently. At 6 feet, a typical conger eel can rip off a person's hand and cause other mutilating wounds. Beachcombers must also beware of the conger eel. It is known to swim into shallow estuaries, where it crawls through the mud, looking for food. Conger eels are also found around coral reefs, but never in water more than 600 feet deep.

Conger eels eat just about anything they can catch. They also feed on dead fish and other animals floating in the sea or lying on the bottom of shallow bays. Like moray eels, conger eels have a very large mouth. But unlike morays, congers have no fangs. They bite evenly with a mouthful of teeth that form a smooth cutting edge.

When they mate, conger eels release large numbers of eggs and sperm into the water. The fertilized eggs float freely with the currents until they hatch into leaf-shaped larvae. These immature eels do not swallow food. Instead, they absorb nutrients from the water directly through their skin. When they are large enough, the larvae sink to the bottom and transform into tiny conger eels. Even as adults, these eels have no scales. They are covered instead with a thick, leathery skin.

Forest Elephant
Loxodonta africana cyclotis

Height at the Shoulder: 7 to 8 feet
Weight: 3 to 5 tons
Diet: mainly grass; also other plant matter

Number of Young: 1
Home: western Africa
Order: Elephants
Family: Elephants

 Rainforests

 Mammals

© MARTIN HARVEY / CORBIS

 Endangered Animals

The forest elephant is one of two subspecies of African elephant. It is smaller than the other subspecies, the savanna elephant, and has longer, straighter tusks. Tusks are very long incisor teeth that are positioned on each side of the jaw. The elephant uses its tusks as a weapon and as a tool for digging in the dirt.

The most important part of the forest elephant's body is its trunk. The trunk allows the elephant to reach tasty plant matter high up in trees and bring this food to its mouth. The elephant uses its trunk to suck up large amounts of water, which it squirts into its mouth. The trunk is also the elephant's organ of smell. And when the creature senses danger, it may strike its trunk on the ground. This warns other elephants in its group that an enemy is near.

Some of the forest elephant's favorite foods are tender young twigs and branches. Sometimes the most tender limbs are high up on a tree, out of the forest elephant's reach. The creature has a quick way to solve the problem. It uses its head as a battering ram, pushing over the tree. It then enjoys dinner at its own level.

A group of forest elephants can cause quite a lot of damage in an area. As soon as one spot is stripped of vegetation, the elephants travel single file to another part of the forest.

Peacock Featherworm
Sabella pavonina

Length: 2 to 4 inches
Weight: about ¹⁄₁₀ ounce
Diet: phytoplankton and organic debris
Method of Reproduction: egg layer

Home: Mediterranean Sea and the coast of Europe
Order: Sabellida
Family: Sabellidae
Subclass: Sedentary tube worms

Oceans and Shores

Other Invertebrates

© ROBERT PICKETT / CORBIS

When you look at a peacock featherworm, your attention is immediately drawn to its spectacular crown. This frilly, colorful crown is actually two half-circles of tentacles. The tentacles are the featherworm's only moving parts. It eats with them. It breathes with them. It even uses them to watch for enemies.

A peacock featherworm's tentacles are constantly brushing the water in search of plankton and dead bits of plants and animals. As the tentacles comb this food out of the water, they sort the combed material according to size and taste. The food that is too big or distasteful to eat gets thrown back. The tasty, bite-sized bits are

swallowed. The worm's feathery tentacles are also gills. That is, the tentacles absorb oxygen from the water, just as our lungs take in oxygen from the air.

Scattered through the featherworm's crown of tentacles are 40 to 50 eyes. The worm cannot see details, in the way a person can. But the worm's primitive eyes can detect shadows and sense motion. This enables the peacock featherworm to sense when a hungry fish or other predator comes near. The worm can't crawl or swim. But it can escape danger by snapping its tender tentacles back inside its tough, leathery tube. The featherworm keeps most of its tubular body buried safely in the sand.

Orange-spotted Filefish
Oxymonacanthus longirostris

Length: about 4 inches
Diet: staghorn coral
Method of Reproduction: egg layer

Home: Indo-Pacific seas
Order: Puffers
Family: Leatherjackets
Subfamily: Filefishes

Oceans and Shores

Fish

© CASEY & ASTRID WITTE MAHANEY / LONELY PLANET IMAGES

The orange-spotted filefish is a wildly colorful fish with small, sharp fangs that protrude from its mouth like a parrot's beak. Even stranger, its eyes can move independently from one another. As its eyes roll in different directions, the fish resembles a crazed cartoon clown. Each eye is surrounded by an orange ring crossed by six blue bars.

The orange-spotted filefish's scales are small and spiny, and fit closely together like flexible armor. The edges of the fish's scales don't overlap, as is usually the case. The gaps between the scales give the filefish an especially prickly texture. To the touch, it feels like rough leather.

The filefish's teeth are designed for nibbling coral animals called polyps. The fish gather in small groups of two to three pairs, always near large, branching colonies of staghorn coral. Drifting from one coral stand to another, the fish nips at the soft coral animals, which try to hide in their hard, cup-shaped shells. Normally filefish swim by weakly rippling their fins. However, they can race away for a short burst when chased. When danger is near, these fish usually retreat deep within the crevices of the coral reef. They commonly nest at the base of the coral, often on small clumps of algae. Orange-spotted filefish are especially common in the tide pools of Australia's Great Barrier Reef.

Snow Finch
Montifringilla nivalis

Length: 7 inches
Number of Eggs: 4 or 5
Home: southern Europe and
Central Asia

Diet: insects and seeds
Order: Perching birds
Family: Weavers

 Forests and
Mountains

 Birds

© KONRAD WOTHE / MINDEN PICTURES

The plump, white-bellied snow finch is a favorite among alpine skiers who trek through the mountains of Europe and Russia. A bold and friendly bird, it is quick to appear, begging for crumbs whenever skiers and hikers stop to make camp.

Snow finches seldom descend from the barren mountaintops except during very harsh winter weather. Small flocks may flee snowstorms by taking refuge in alpine valleys. But as soon as the clouds clear, the birds return to their home above the tree line. These hardy finches survive by hunting for insects on bare rocks and dirt. In summer and early fall, they gorge on the seeds of alpine grasses and herbs.

Snow finches are often seen perching on rocks and buildings, flicking their tail nervously. Their call is a short, harsh "tswik, tswik." Snow finches sing more melodiously while flying, especially during mating season in the spring. Their flight song alternates between a rapid trilling and a repeated, lyrical phrase: "sitticher-sitticher."

After mating in spring, male and female snow finches work together to build a simple nest inside a rock crevice, an abandoned animal burrow, or on the ledge of a building. They make a soft, warm bed of feathers, hair, dead grass, and moss, onto which the female lays her eggs. The parents take turns warming the nest for the next two weeks and share in feeding the new chicks.

Water Flea (Daphnia)
Daphnia sp.

Length: less than ¼ inch
Diet: one-celled organisms and organic matter
Method of Reproduction: eggs that develop and hatch inside the mother

Home: worldwide in ponds and other quiet freshwater habitats
Order: Water fleas
Family: Daphnias

Fresh Water

Arthropods

© ROBERT PICKETT / CORBIS

Through a microscope, you can actually watch the daphnia's heart beating, see food moving through its digestive tract, or even see unborn daphnia developing within the mother's special brood chamber! All these sights are possible because the daphnia's body is transparent, making it easy to see its internal body parts. The daphnia's external body parts include two long, branched antennae, which always move swiftly back and forth. This action causes the daphnia to jerk its way about the water.

Daphnias are very common—and very tiny. So tiny, in fact, that they were not discovered by people until the first microscopes were developed. In 1669 the Dutch scientist Jan Swammerdam became the first person to describe daphnias. Because they seemed to hop about all the time, he called them "water fleas." These "fleas," however, don't attack dogs!

Daphnias are among the most important animals in their quiet freshwater habitats. They are eaten by many little fish and other animals, which are in turn eaten by larger animals. This transfer of food energy from one kind of organism to another is called a food chain. If one "link" in the food chain disappears, animals farther up the chain starve. Therefore, the daphnia, which is close to the bottom of the food chain, is extremely important for the survival of all the many animals above it on the chain.

Red-shafted Flicker
Colaptes auratus cafer

Length: 10 to 14 inches
Weight: about 5 ounces
Diet: mainly ants; also other insects, acorns, grain, fruits, and berries

Number of Eggs: 5 to 8
Home: western North America
Order: Woodpeckers, toucans, and honeyguides
Family: Woodpeckers

 Forests and Mountains

 Birds

Although a type of woodpecker, the western North American red-shafted flicker spends little time in the trees. Instead, it finds its food on the ground, pecking ants off the soil and licking them from tree branches. Its wood-pecking skills come into play only during the mating season. To attract a female, the male drums his bill, usually on a tree, but occasionally on a sheet-metal roof. During this rather noisy courtship, the birds also conduct elaborate mating rituals, facing each other, bobbing about, and flashing the brilliant red undersides of their wings and tails.

Once courtship has ended, the male finds a nest site—preferably a tree cavity or a wooden birdhouse. If such ideal housing is not readily available, the red-shafted flickers again call upon their chiseling skills, this time to drill a nest hole in a tree, telephone pole, or even a cactus. Both birds take turns incubating the creamy-white eggs, which hatch in about two weeks.

A related subspecies, the yellow-shafted flicker, sports golden-yellow feathers under its wings and tail. This flicker lives in the eastern United States and Canada. The ranges of the two varieties overlap along the western edge of the Great Plains. In that area that flickers often interbreed, producing young with orange under-feathers.

Common Liver Fluke
Fasciola hepatica

Length: about ⅘ of an inch
Diet: living tissue
Method of Reproduction: egg layer

Home: worldwide
Order: Neorhabdocoela
Family: Fasciolids

 Fresh Water

© SINCLAIR STAMMERS / SPL / PHOTO RESEARCHERS

Other
Invertebrates

The common liver fluke is a worm that infects mammals, including people. This parasite is a problem throughout the world. It is most common in areas where sheep and cattle are raised and are often infected.

The life of a liver fluke begins when the parasite's eggs are passed out with an infected animal's or person's droppings, or feces. The eggs are invisible to the naked eye. When an egg gets into water, it hatches into a larva that infects an aquatic snail. Inside the snail, its first host, the developing liver fluke changes body shape two times and then produces germ balls. The germ balls hatch into a new kind of larva called a cercaria, which has a long tail. The cercaria, still too small to see, escapes from the snail's body, back into the water. It attaches itself to underwater plants and forms a hard case, or cyst, around its body.

When a person or animal eats one of the infested plants, such as watercress, he or she becomes the liver fluke's second host. Inside its host's intestines, the liver fluke breaks out of its cyst and burrows to the liver, on which it feeds.

In addition to causing liver disease in people, liver flukes have an economic impact. About $3 million worth of calves' liver is destroyed each year because fluke infections have made the meat unfit to eat.

Large Bee Fly
Bombylius major

Length: 0.3 to 0.5 inch
Diet: nectar and pollen (adult); bee eggs and larvae (larva)
Method of Reproduction: egg layer

Home: northern temperate regions of Europe, Asia, and North America
Order: Flies and mosquitoes
Family: Bee flies

 Grasslands

 Arthropods

© BOB GOSSINGTON / BRUCE COLEMAN INC.

It is easy to mistake the large bee fly for a bee. The bee fly has a stout body that is densely covered with long yellow and black hairs—just like the fuzzy body of a bee. The bee fly's long, slender mouthparts are designed for eating nectar and pollen—just like the mouthparts of a bee. But the bee fly has only one pair of wings; a bee has two.

Large bee flies are often seen on warm spring days in fields and sunny places near the edge of woodlands. They hover in one spot for a few seconds, then dart a short distance to a new position. When a bee fly spots a likely source of nectar and pollen, it settles onto the edge of the flower and begins to feed.

Bee flies depend on bees for their life cycle. Some bee species live in colonies. Others, called solitary bees, live alone. When a female bee fly spots a female solitary bee, she follows it as it flies from flower to flower and finally back to its nest. Then the bee fly waits patiently until the bee leaves her home. Once no one's home, the large bee fly lays her eggs in the entrance to the bee's nest. The eggs hatch into larvae and feed on pollen stored in the bee's nest. When the larvae grow bigger and develop mouthparts, they eat the bee's eggs and larvae. When bee-fly larvae reach their full size, they enter the pupa stage and change into adults.

Fork-tailed Flycatcher
Muscivora tyrannus

Length of the Body: 5 to 7 inches
Length of the Tail: 7 to 9 inches
Diet: mainly insects

Number of Eggs: 4 to 6
Home: Central and South America
Order: Perching birds
Family: Tyrant flycatchers

Cities, Towns, and Farms

Birds

© LAWRENCE E. NAYLOR / PHOTO RESEARCHERS

A fork-tailed flycatcher sits motionless on a high fence wire. Only its eyes move as the bird scans the ground and sky for insects. Then, suddenly, the large flycatcher swoops down on a fat grasshopper and tears its meal apart with its strong, hooked bill.

When it flies, the fork-tailed flycatcher opens its two long tail feathers like a pair of scissors. Its long tail helps the bird maneuver as it chases after elusive insects. When it perches, the fork-tailed flycatcher neatly refolds its tail feathers, one over the other.

The fork-tailed flycatcher is a member of the largest bird family in the world. There are more than 400 species of tyrant flycatchers, all of them in the Americas.

Several of the fork-tailed flycatcher's closest relatives also have long scissor tails. You can tell this species from the others by its black crown. If you could get close enough to part this bird's head feathers, you would find a hidden patch of tiny yellow fluff in the middle of its crown.

Male and female fork-tailed flycatchers mate for life. The male defends the pair's territory from other flycatchers. The female has the job of warming their eggs and young. Both parents share in feeding the growing chicks and teaching them how to hunt. The young are usually ready for independence a few months after leaving the nest. They will find their own mates the following year.

African Bat-eared Fox
Otocyon megalotis

Length: 20 to 24 inches
Length of the Tail: 12 to 14 inches
Weight: 7 to 10 pounds
Diet: insects, lizards, eggs, fruits, and small animals

Number of Young: 1 to 5
Home: southwestern and east-central Africa
Order: Carnivores
Family: Dogs

 Grasslands

 Mammals

© PETER JOHNSON / CORBIS

It's easy to see how the African bat-eared fox got its name. Even its scientific name—*megalotis*—means "giant ears." This tiny fox puts its "bat" ears to good use when hunting insects and mice. It can hear a grasshopper flapping its wings, a termite digging a tunnel, or a mouse tiptoeing through the grass. African farmers are grateful for the way the bat-eared fox gobbles up mice and insects before these pests can damage crops.

The African bat-eared fox generally avoids moving about during the day, for fear of attack by large predatory birds. The only time this fox hunts by daylight is when it has a den of hungry babies, called whelps, to feed. When the parent foxes arrive home after a hunting trip, their tiny young scurry out of their den. Their father and mother regurgitate a partly digested meal of insects. If the hunting has been especially good, they may carry home a lizard, bird, or other small animal.

Once the whelps are half-grown, their parents resume their nocturnal ways. They lead their young out in the evening and teach them to find insects and other small creatures to eat. The young foxes learn to locate their prey precisely, by first listening with one ear and then turning their heads to listen with the other. They become independent and go their separate ways when they are about 10 months old.

Colpeo Fox
Dusicyon culpaeus

Length of the Body: 2 to 3¾ feet
Length of the Tail: 14 to 16 inches
Height at the Shoulder: about 16 inches
Weight: 9 to 26 pounds

Diet: plants, fruits, reptiles, rodents, rabbits, and sheep
Number of Young: 3 to 6
Home: western South America
Order: Carnivores
Family: Dogs

 Forests and Mountains

 Mammals

© ROLAND SEITRE / PETER ARNOLD, INC.

Like the familiar red fox of North America, the colpeo fox is long and lean with a thick, bushy tail. But not all colpeo foxes look alike.

At the northern tip of their range, where the climate is warm, colpeo foxes are small, no bigger than a beagle. But high in the Andes Mountains and at the southern end of South America, colpeo foxes grow bigger as the climate grows colder. At the snowy tip of Argentina—not too far from Antarctica—colpeo foxes are nearly as big as wolves and wear thick fur coats. Colpeo foxes that live in cold climates also have larger and stronger jaws and teeth. This enables them to catch bigger meals.

Colpeo foxes prefer to live alone most of the year. But in August, they yearn for company. They howl, day and night, until each finds a mate. Once they have bred, mated pairs stay together for nearly five months. First they find a den where the female can give birth—perhaps a rocky cave or just a thick clump of bushes. Then, hunting as a team, the couple gather food and hide it near the den. Once the young are born, the parents guard them fearlessly, chasing away any intruder, no matter how large. By October, when they are two months old, the young foxes are strong enough to follow their parents and learn how to hunt. By January the close-knit family splits up, each member going its separate way.

Agile Frog
Rana dalmatina

Length of the Adult: 4⅜ inches

Length of the Tadpole: up to 2¼ inches

Diet of the Adult: insects

Diet of the Tadpole: algae

Number of Eggs: 669 to 1,415

Home: Central and southeastern Europe

Order: Frogs and toads

Family: True frogs

Fresh Water

Amphibians

© J.C. CARTON / BRUCE COLEMAN INC.

The agile frog takes its name from its spectacular jumping ability. It is considered to be the best jumper in Europe, where it is a common inhabitant of forests and meadows.

In early spring, male agile frogs can be heard rapidly calling for their mates with a loud "ko-ko-ko." Once she has mated, a female frog lays a large clump of eggs in a pond.

Agile tadpoles hatch between March and May. For the next three months, they swim along the bottom of ponds, gobbling up algae. The tadpoles use their mouth to filter out unwanted mud and water. Agile tadpoles grow quickly until they are ready to change, or metamorphose, into adult frogs. Gradually, they grow legs as their tails shrink and disappear. The maturing tadpoles change on the inside, too. They develop air-inhaling lungs at the same time as they lose the gills they once used to "breathe" oxygen from water.

Finally, in July or August, agile tadpoles are ready to leave the pond and live as frogs. As adults, this species spends less time in the water than do other frogs. But they need moist ground and a thick cover of plants to keep from drying out. In fall, agile frogs return to their ponds, bury themselves in the mud, and close their eyes for a deep winter sleep.

Set Index